# Mighty Fun

# Multiplication

## PRACTICE PUZZLES

## 40 Reproducible Solve-the-Riddle Activity Pages
## That Help All Kids Master Multiplication

by Bob Hugel

SCHOLASTIC
PROFESSIONAL BOOKS

# Dedication

To Leah and Donovan

Cover and interior design by
**Holly Grundon**

Illustrations by
**Elwood Smith**

**ISBN # 0-439-07754-0**
Copyright © 2001 by Bob Hugel
Printed in the U.S.A.

# Contents

# Introduction

Welcome to *Mighty Fun Multiplication Practice Puzzles*, a surefire book that combines basic multiplication problems with loads of hilarious riddles guaranteed to get students revved up for learning.

As you may already know, one of the keys to helping students learn successfully is to make learning fun. That's why each page of *Mighty Fun Multiplication Practice Puzzles* starts with an amusing riddle. We hope your students will be motivated to solve the multiplication problems to help them find the rib-tickling answer to each riddle.

Along the way, your students will get drilled on several multiplication skills, including practicing the times tables 1 to 10, multiplying 1- to 4-digit numbers, fractions, and decimals, as well as solving measurement, time, and word problems. We hope your students enjoy *Mighty Fun Multiplication Practice Puzzles* and benefit from the skills presented in this book.

By making multiplication enjoyable, we hope to reveal a terrific secret to your students—math is lots of fun!

NAME _____

## Riddle 1

# What did the rocket say when it left the party?

## What To Do

To find the answer to the riddle, solve the multiplication problems. Then, match each product with a letter in the Key below. Write the correct letters on the blanks below.

**1**   5 x 1 = _____

**2**   8 x 1 = _____

**3**   11 x 1 = _____

**4**   26 x 1 = _____

**5**   3 x 2 = _____

**6**   5 x 2 = _____

**7**   6 x 2 = _____

**8**   8 x 2 = _____

**9**   9 x 2 = _____

**10**   12 x 2 = _____

## Key

| | | |
|---|---|---|
| 10 .......... F | 27 .......... U | 20 .......... W |
| 13 .......... C | 8 .......... E | 7 .......... D |
| 11 .......... O | 6 .......... K | 12 .......... T |
| 16 .......... E | 9 .......... B | 26 .......... O |
| 5 .......... A | 24 .......... F | 18 .......... T |

**Riddle Answer:** "TIM ___ ___ ___ ___ ___ ___ ___ ___ ___ ___."

NAME _____

## Riddle 2

# What did the owl say when someone knocked on its door?

## What To Do

To find the answer to the riddle, solve the multiplication problems. Then, match each product with a letter in the Key below. Write the correct letters on the blanks below.

**1** 5 x 3 = _____

**2** 2 x 3 = _____

**3** 8 x 3 = _____

**4** 4 x 3 = _____

**5** 9 x 3 = _____

**6** 6 x 3 = _____

**7** 10 x 3 = _____

**8** 12 x 3 = _____

**9** 11 x 3 = _____

**10** 0 x 3 = _____

## Key

| | | |
|---|---|---|
| 30 . . . . . . . . . O | 8 . . . . . . . . . K | 42 . . . . . . . . . N |
| 11 . . . . . . . . . A | 15 . . . . . . . . . O | 24 . . . . . . . . . T |
| 36 . . . . . . . . . H | 0 . . . . . . . . . I | 33 . . . . . . . . . O |
| 18 . . . . . . . . . I | 27 . . . . . . . . . O | 6 . . . . . . . . . Q |
| 32 . . . . . . . . . F | 6 . . . . . . . . . S | 12 . . . . . . . . . W |

Riddle
Answer: " ___ ___ ___ ___ ___ ___   ___ ___   ___ ___ ?"
        **4** **8** **5** **9** **1** **7**  **10** **2**  **6** **3**

NAME _____

## Riddle 3

# What does a basketball player never have to pay for?

## What To Do

To find the answer to the riddle, solve the multiplication problems. Then, match each product with a letter in the Key below. Write the correct letters on the blanks below.

**1** 3 x 4 = _____

**2** 6 x 4 = _____

**3** 2 x 4 = _____

**4** 9 x 4 = _____

**5** 7 x 4 = _____

**6** 10 x 4 = _____

**7** 8 x 4 = _____

**8** 13 x 4 = _____

**9** 1 x 4 = _____

**10** 12 x 4 = _____

## Key

| | | |
|---|---|---|
| 11 . . . . . . . . . I | 48 . . . . . . . . . R | 23 . . . . . . . . . G |
| 24 . . . . . . . . . E | 40 . . . . . . . . . A | 32 . . . . . . . . . W |
| 36 . . . . . . . . . H | 52 . . . . . . . . . F | 4 . . . . . . . . . E |
| 28 . . . . . . . . . R | 7 . . . . . . . . . N | 50 . . . . . . . . . D |
| 12 . . . . . . . . . T | 8 . . . . . . . . . O | 22 . . . . . . . . . C |

Riddle
Answer:

___ " ___ ___ ___ ___ " ___ ___ ___ ___ ___
**6**     **8** **5** **2** **9**     **1** **4** **10** **3** **7**

NAME _____

## Riddle 4

# What always has an eye out for entertainment?

## What To Do

To find the answer to the riddle, solve the multiplication problems. Then, match each product with a letter in the Key below. Write the correct letters on the blanks below.

**1** 4 x 5 = _____

**2** 6 x 5 = _____

**3** 10 x 5 = _____

**4** 8 x 5 = _____

**5** 12 x 5 = _____

**6** 15 x 5 = _____

**7** 20 x 5 = _____

**8** 25 x 5 = _____

**9** 30 x 5 = _____

**10** 5 x 5 = _____

## Key

| | | |
|---|---|---|
| 120 . . . . . . . . . B | 125 . . . . . . . . . E | 150 . . . . . . . . . E |
| 40 . . . . . . . . . L | 60 . . . . . . . . . T | 100 . . . . . . . . . N |
| 85 . . . . . . . . . M | 20 . . . . . . . . . I | 45 . . . . . . . . . U |
| 25 . . . . . . . . . V | 70 . . . . . . . . . W | 50 . . . . . . . . . O |
| 30 . . . . . . . . . I | 75 . . . . . . . . . S | 90 . . . . . . . . . J |

Riddle
Answer: ___ ___ ___ ___ " ___ ___ ___ ___ ___ ___ "
    **5** **9** **4** **8** **10** **2** **6** **1** **3** **7**

NAME _____

Riddle 5

# Why did the car make so much noise?

## What To Do

To find the answer to the riddle, solve the multiplication problems. Then, match each product with a letter in the Key below. Write the correct letters on the blanks below.

**1**   2 x 6 = _____     **6**   3 x 6 = _____

**2**   8 x 6 = _____     **7**   9 x 6 = _____

**3**   4 x 6 = _____     **8**   12 x 6 = _____

**4**   10 x 6 = _____     **9**   7 x 6 = _____

**5**   15 x 6 = _____     **10**   20 x 6 = _____

## Key

| | | |
|---|---|---|
| 18 . . . . . . . . . O | 112 . . . . . . . . . A | 120 . . . . . . . . . T |
| 42 . . . . . . . . . R | 12 . . . . . . . . . U | 15 . . . . . . . . . P |
| 60 . . . . . . . . . T | 21 . . . . . . . . . G | 123 . . . . . . . . . W |
| 90 . . . . . . . . . O | 48 . . . . . . . . . M | 72 . . . . . . . . . H |
| 10 . . . . . . . . . F | 24 . . . . . . . . . M | 54 . . . . . . . . . O |

Riddle Answer:   **IT HAD A**   __ __ __ __ __   __ __ __ __ __ .

                   **3**   **7**   **10**   **6**   **9**     **2**   **5**   **1**   **4**   **8**

NAME _____

## Riddle 6

# Why did the puppy fall asleep?

## What To Do

To find the answer to the riddle, solve the multiplication problems. Then, match each product with a letter in the Key below. Write the correct letters on the blanks below.

1. $6 \times 7 =$ _____

2. $10 \times 7 =$ _____

3. $7 \times 7 =$ _____

4. $12 \times 7 =$ _____

5. $8 \times 7 =$ _____

6. $5 \times 7 =$ _____

7. $2 \times 7 =$ _____

8. $11 \times 7 =$ _____

9. $3 \times 7 =$ _____

10. $9 \times 7 =$ _____

## Key

| | | | | | |
|---|---|---|---|---|---|
| 56 ........ R | 77 ........ G | 84 ........ O |
| 21 ........ D | 17 ........ W | 49 ........ E |
| 13 ........ U | 63 ........ D | 9 ........ P |
| 70 ........ S | 7 ........ H | 35 ........ A |
| 14 ........ I | 42 ........ T | 18 ........ N |

Riddle Answer:   IT W ___ ___   ___ ___ ___   ___ ___ ___ ___ ___.

6  2      10  4  8      1  7  5  3  9

NAME _____

## Riddle 7

# What kind of pie do ghosts like best?

YUM!

## What To Do

To find the answer to the riddle, solve the multiplication problems. Then, match each product with a letter in the Key below. Write the correct letters on the blanks below.

**1** 2 x 8 = _____   **6** 10 x 8 = _____

**2** 6 x 8 = _____   **7** 9 x 8 = _____

**3** 3 x 8 = _____   **8** 5 x 8 = _____

**4** 8 x 8 = _____   **9** 14 x 8 = _____

**5** 4 x 8 = _____   **10** 11 x 8 = _____

## Key

| | | | | | |
|---|---|---|---|---|---|
| 80 ......... B | 24 ......... R | 40 ......... O |
| 10 ......... Q | 12 ......... K | 112 ......... P |
| 16 ......... E | 64 ......... I | 120 ......... N |
| 72 ......... Y | 48 ......... O | 32 ......... R |
| 23 ......... T | 88 ......... E | 8 ......... G |

## Riddle Answer:

"B __ __" __ __ __ __ __   __ __ __
   **8** **2**  **6** **1** **5** **3** **7**  **9** **4** **10**

NAME _____

### Riddle 8

# Why did the dog chew up the wooden table leg?

## What To Do

To find the answer to the riddle, solve the multiplication problems. Then, match each product with a letter in the Key below. Write the correct letters on the blanks below.

**1** 10 x 9 = _____

**2** 1 x 9 = _____

**3** 4 x 9 = _____

**4** 13 x 9 = _____

**5** 8 x 9 = _____

**6** 9 x 9 = _____

**7** 6 x 9 = _____

**8** 5 x 9 = _____

**9** 7 x 9 = _____

**10** 20 x 9 = _____

## Key

| | | | | | |
|---|---|---|---|---|---|
| 54 . . . . . . . . R | | 81 . . . . . . . . S | | 90 . . . . . . . . K | |
| 180 . . . . . . . . D | | 9 . . . . . . . . O | | 45 . . . . . . . . E | |
| 120 . . . . . . . . I | | 48 . . . . . . . . T | | 72 . . . . . . . . B | |
| 188 . . . . . . . . G | | 99 . . . . . . . . Q | | 63 . . . . . . . . M | |
| 117 . . . . . . . . E | | 36 . . . . . . . . A | | 21 . . . . . . . . L | |

### Riddle Answer:

**IT WANT** __ __  __ __ __ __ __ " __ __ __ __."

       **4** **10**   **6** **2** **9** **8**   **5** **3** **7** **1**

NAME _____

## Riddle 9

# What should you take on a trip to the desert?

## What To Do

To find the answer to the riddle, solve the multiplication problems. Then, match each product with a letter in the Key below. Write the correct letters on the blanks below.

**1**  4 x 10  = _____      **6**  14 x 100 = _____

**2**  7 x 10  = _____      **7**  6 x 100 = _____

**3**  10 x 10  = _____      **8**  30 x 100 = _____

**4**  12 x 10  = _____      **9**  50 x 100 = _____

**5**  36 x 10  = _____      **10**  75 x 100 = _____

## Key

| | | |
|---|---|---|
| 70 .........T | 750 .........U | 40 .........S |
| 500 .........B | 360 .........I | 60 .........Q |
| 140 .........C | 600 .........T | 3,000 .........K |
| 7,500 .........A | 1,000 .........O | 120 .........I |
| 100 .........I | 5,000 .........R | 1,400 .........D |

## Riddle Answer:

A  "TH __ __ __ __ __"- __ __ __  __ __ __
   **3** **9** **1** **7**  **10** **4** **6**  **8** **5** **2**

NAME _____

## Riddle 10

# What are a bandit's favorite fruits?

## What To Do

To find the answer to the riddle, solve the multiplication problems. Then, match each product with a letter in the Key below. Write the correct letters on the blanks below.

**1** 1 x 1 = _____

**2** 2 x 2 = _____

**3** 3 x 3 = _____

**4** 4 x 4 = _____

**5** 5 x 5 = _____

**6** 6 x 6 = _____

**7** 7 x 7 = _____

**8** 8 x 8 = _____

**9** 9 x 9 = _____

## Key

| | | |
|---|---|---|
| 16 . . . . . . . . L | 4 . . . . . . . . P | 30 . . . . . . . . I |
| 100 . . . . . . . . X | 22 . . . . . . . . C | 49 . . . . . . . . P |
| 36 . . . . . . . . S | 25 . . . . . . . . B | 8 . . . . . . . . W |
| 1 . . . . . . . . A | 14 . . . . . . . . U | 81 . . . . . . . . D |
| 64 . . . . . . . . E | 9 . . . . . . . . A | 42 . . . . . . . . H |

Riddle
Answer: ___ ___ ___   ___ ___ ___ ___ ___ ___
**5** **1** **9**   **3** **7** **2** **4** **8** **6**

NAME _____

## Riddle 11

# What kinds of food are popular at the beach?

## What To Do

To find the answer to the riddle, solve the multiplication problems. Then, match each product with a letter in the Key below. Write the correct letters on the blanks below.

**1** 10 x 10 = _____

**2** 11 x 11 = _____

**3** 12 x 12 = _____

**4** 13 x 13 = _____

**5** 14 x 14 = _____

**6** 15 x 15 = _____

**7** 16 x 16 = _____

**8** 17 x 17 = _____

**9** 18 x 18 = _____

**10** 19 x 19 = _____

## Key

| | | |
|---|---|---|
| 222 .........B | 196 .........D | 256 .........A |
| 169 .........S | 111 .........U | 342 .........Z |
| 121 .........I | 225 .........C | 289 .........H |
| 324 .........S | 100 .........N | 256 .........K |
| 144 .........E | 112 .........Y | 361 .........W |

## Riddle Answer:

" ___ ___ ___ " ___ ___ ___ ___ ___ ___
**4** **7** **1** **5** **10** **2** **6** **8** **3** **9**

NAME _____

## Riddle 12

# Where did the turkey, ham, and roast beef go to party?

## What To Do

To find the answer to the riddle, solve the multiplication problems. Then, match each product with a letter in the Key below. Write the correct letters on the blanks below.

**1** 30 x 6 = _____

**2** 60 x 5 = _____

**3** 50 x 8 = _____

**4** 40 x 4 = _____

**5** 70 x 3 = _____

**6** 80 x 7 = _____

**7** 90 x 9 = _____

**8** 45 x 2 = _____

**9** 35 x 5 = _____

## Key

| | | |
|---|---|---|
| 175 . . . . . . . . . T | 300 . . . . . . . . . E | 650 . . . . . . . . . N |
| 560 . . . . . . . . . A | 100 . . . . . . . . . I | 90 . . . . . . . . . M |
| 190 . . . . . . . . . O | 810 . . . . . . . . . A | 180 . . . . . . . . . A |
| 160 . . . . . . . . . L | 80 . . . . . . . . . P | 840 . . . . . . . . . D |
| 210 . . . . . . . . . L | 400 . . . . . . . . . B | 250 . . . . . . . . . G |

Riddle
Answer:  ____ " ____ ____ ____ ____ " ____ ____ ____ ____
　　　　　**1**　　**8** **2** **7** **9**　　**3** **6** **4** **5**

NAME _____

## Riddle 13

# What did the doctor say to the patient who swallowed a roll of film?

## What To Do

To find the answer to the riddle, solve the multiplication problems. Then, match each product with a letter in the Key below. Write the correct letters on the blanks below.

**1** 15 x 2 = _____

**2** 14 x 3 = _____

**3** 13 x 5 = _____

**4** 11 x 7 = _____

**5** 18 x 4 = _____

**6** 12 x 4 = _____

**7** 16 x 5 = _____

**8** 19 x 2 = _____

**9** 17 x 7 = _____

**10** 15 x 8 = _____

## Key

| 119 . . . . . . . . S | 38 . . . . . . . . O | 122 . . . . . . . . W |
| 52 . . . . . . . . U | 63 . . . . . . . . D | 65 . . . . . . . . P |
| 72 . . . . . . . . L | 80 . . . . . . . . G | 42 . . . . . . . . E |
| 115 . . . . . . . . P | 48 . . . . . . . . N | 77 . . . . . . . . D |
| 30 . . . . . . . . E | 46 . . . . . . . . L | 120 . . . . . . . . V |

Riddle
Answer:     "HOPE NOTHI __ __    __ __ __ __ __ __ __ __."
                         **6** **7**   **4** **1** **10** **2** **5** **8** **3** **9**

NAME _____

## Riddle 14

# Why do spiders use computers?

## What To Do

To find the answer to the riddle, solve the multiplication problems. Then, match each product with a letter in the Key below. Write the correct letters on the blanks below.

**1** 200 x 8 = _____

**2** 400 x 6 = _____

**3** 500 x 3 = _____

**4** 100 x 9 = _____

**5** 600 x 8 = _____

**6** 300 x 6 = _____

**7** 700 x 4 = _____

**8** 800 x 5 = _____

**9** 500 x 7 = _____

**10** 900 x 3 = _____

## Key

| | | |
|---|---|---|
| 1,600 . . . . . . . . . S | 2,200 . . . . . . . . . K | 1,000 . . . . . . . . . V |
| 2,400 . . . . . . . . . W | 4,800 . . . . . . . . . T | 4,000 . . . . . . . . . T |
| 1,800 . . . . . . . . . B | 1,500 . . . . . . . . . S | 3,500 . . . . . . . . . E |
| 1,200 . . . . . . . . . F | 2,000 . . . . . . . . . G | 2,700 . . . . . . . . . I |
| 900 . . . . . . . . . E | 2,800 . . . . . . . . . I | 3,200 . . . . . . . . . L |

Riddle
Answer:   **TO   VIS** __ __  " __ __ __ "  __ __ __ __ __

   **10** **5**   **2** **9** **6**   **3** **7** **8** **4** **1**

NAME _____

## Riddle 15

# What kind of cat is the life of the party?

## What To Do

To find the answer to the riddle, solve the multiplication problems. Then, match each product with a letter in the Key below. Write the correct letters on the blanks below.

**1** 110 x 3 = _____

**2** 160 x 4 = _____

**3** 220 x 6 = _____

**4** 250 x 2 = _____

**5** 330 x 7 = _____

**6** 340 x 8 = _____

**7** 420 x 9 = _____

**8** 450 x 5 = _____

## Key

| | | | | | |
|---|---|---|---|---|---|
| 1,320 | A | 640 | D | 2,520 | R |
| 2,270 | O | 350 | K | 500 | A |
| 3,780 | T | 330 | W | 2,130 | X |
| 1,230 | P | 450 | S | 2,720 | C |
| 2,250 | L | 2,310 | I | 1,000 | B |

**Riddle Answer:**

___  "___ ___ ___ ___"  ___ ___ ___
④      ①  ⑤  ⑧  ②      ⑥  ③  ⑦

NAME _____

### Riddle 16

# Why did the bowling pins lie down?

## What To Do

To find the answer to the riddle, solve the multiplication problems. Then, match each product with a letter in the Key below. Write the correct letters on the blanks below.

**1** 111 x 1 = _____

**2** 120 x 9 = _____

**3** 212 x 7 = _____

**4** 189 x 6 = _____

**5** 306 x 5 = _____

**6** 476 x 6 = _____

**7** 522 x 8 = _____

**8** 382 x 4 = _____

**9** 769 x 2 = _____

**10** 647 x 3 = _____

## Key

| | | |
|---|---|---|
| 1,941 . . . . . . . . . T | 1,008 . . . . . . . . . A | 111 . . . . . . . . . N |
| 1,583 . . . . . . . . . U | 2,856 . . . . . . . . . K | 1,538 . . . . . . . . . E |
| 1,134 . . . . . . . . . O | 1,143 . . . . . . . . . B | 1,528 . . . . . . . . . S |
| 1,548 . . . . . . . . . W | 4,176 . . . . . . . . . R | 10,000 . . . . . . . . . X |
| 1,484 . . . . . . . . . I | 1,080 . . . . . . . . . T | 1,530 . . . . . . . . . N |

Riddle
Answer:  **THEY   WE** __ __  __ __   "__ __ __ __ __ __ __"

NAME _____

## Riddle 17

# What are the cheapest ships to buy?

## What To Do

To find the answer to the riddle, solve the multiplication problems. Then, match each product with a letter in the Key below. Write the correct letters on the blanks below.

1  100 x 23 = _____

2  200 x 17 = _____

3  300 x 31 = _____

4  400 x 44 = _____

5  500 x 19 = _____

6  600 x 27 = _____

7  700 x 35 = _____

8  800 x 18 = _____

9  900 x 50 = _____

## Key

| | | |
|---|---|---|
| 3,200 . . . . . . . . D | 16,200 . . . . . . . B | 16,700 . . . . . . . H |
| 17,600 . . . . . . . L | 3,600 . . . . . . . K | 24,500 . . . . . . . O |
| 10,500 . . . . . . . I | 3,400 . . . . . . . T | 12,600 . . . . . . . Y |
| 45,000 . . . . . . . A | 9,300 . . . . . . . E | 14,400 . . . . . . . A |
| 15,300 . . . . . . . R | 9,500 . . . . . . . S | 2,300 . . . . . . . S |

Riddle
Answer:  " ___ ___ ___ ___ " ___ ___ ___ ___ ___
         5   9   4   3     6   7   8   2   1

NAME _____

## Riddle 18

# What do pigs want for dessert?

## What To Do

To find the answer to the riddle, solve the multiplication problems. Then, match each product with a letter in the Key below. Write the correct letters on the blanks below.

**1**  2,000 x 4 = _____

**2**  1,500 x 3 = _____

**3**  3,600 x 2 = _____

**4**  1,300 x 8 = _____

**5**  5,700 x 5 = _____

**6**  2,250 x 1 = _____

**7**  6,600 x 7 = _____

**8**  4,340 x 3 = _____

**9**  1,180 x 9 = _____

**10**  8,620 x 5 = _____

## Key

| | | |
|---|---|---|
| 25,800 . . . . . . . R | 12,300 . . . . . . . G | 7,200 . . . . . . . F |
| 2,250 . . . . . . . S | 10,620 . . . . . . . U | 41,300 . . . . . . . N |
| 43,100 . . . . . . . O | 46,200 . . . . . . . D | 4,500 . . . . . . . E |
| 42,600 . . . . . . . K | 13,020 . . . . . . . S | 10,400 . . . . . . . I |
| 8,000 . . . . . . . M | 28,500 . . . . . . . P | 5,400 . . . . . . . H |

Riddle Answer:   **LOT** __ __ __  __ __ __  __ __ __ __
                       ⑥  ⑩ ③  ① ⑨ ⑦  ⑤ ④ ② ⑧

NAME _____

## Riddle 19

# What kind of dog loves to take baths?

## What To Do

To find the answer to the riddle, solve the multiplication problems. Then, match each product with a letter in the Key below. Write the correct letters on the blanks below.

**1** 1,115 x 6 = _____

**2** 2,323 x 8 = _____

**3** 1,789 x 4 = _____

**4** 3,021 x 9 = _____

**5** 4,476 x 5 = _____

**6** 5,612 x 7 = _____

**7** 6,066 x 8 = _____

**8** 8,126 x 3 = _____

**9** 2,484 x 9 = _____

**10** 7,391 x 6 = _____

## Key

| | | |
|---|---|---|
| 7,156 . . . . . . . . . D | 5,450 . . . . . . . . . D | 48,582 . . . . . . . . . I |
| 39,284 . . . . . . . . . H | 48,528 . . . . . . . . . E | 22,308 . . . . . . . . . O |
| 44,346 . . . . . . . . . O | 18,584 . . . . . . . . . L | 22,380 . . . . . . . . . O |
| 22,830 . . . . . . . . . F | 24,378 . . . . . . . . . M | 22,356 . . . . . . . . . A |
| 6,690 . . . . . . . . . P | 27,189 . . . . . . . . . S | 39,248 . . . . . . . . . G |

Riddle
Answer:   A  "____  ____  ____  ____  ____  ____  ____  ____  ____  ____"
**4** **6** **9** **8** **1** **10** **5** **3** **2** **7**

NAME _____

## Riddle 20

# Why did the spider join the baseball team?

## What To Do

To find the answer to the riddle, solve the multiplication problems. Then, match each product with a letter in the Key below. Write the correct letters on the blanks below.

**1** 1,000 x 11 = _____

**2** 2,000 x 12 = _____

**3** 3,000 x 10 = _____

**4** 4,000 x 14 = _____

**5** 5,000 x 20 = _____

**6** 6,000 x 24 = _____

**7** 7,000 x 30 = _____

**8** 8,000 x 32 = _____

**9** 9,000 x 40 = _____

**10** 7,500 x 50 = _____

## Key

| | | |
|---|---|---|
| 56,000 . . . . . . . H | 65,000 . . . . . . . M | 30,000 . . . . . . . C |
| 11,000 . . . . . . . I | 144,000 . . . . . . . T | 375,000 . . . . . . . C |
| 265,000 . . . . . . B | 25,000 . . . . . . . N | 10,000 . . . . . . . Y |
| 360,000 . . . . . . F | 256,000 . . . . . . . L | 100,000 . . . . . . . A |
| 210,000 . . . . . . E | 90,000 . . . . . . . Q | 24,000 . . . . . . . S |

Riddle Answer: **TO** ___ ___ ___ ___ ___   " ___ ___ ___ ___ ___ "

NAME _____

### Riddle 21

# What did the candle say to the match?

## What To Do

To find the answer to the riddle, solve the multiplication problems. Then, match each product with a letter in the Key below. Write the correct letters on the blanks below.

1. 1 x 1 x 1 = _____
2. 2 x 2 x 2 = _____
3. 3 x 3 x 3 = _____
4. 4 x 4 x 4 = _____
5. 5 x 5 x 5 = _____

6. 6 x 6 x 6 = _____
7. 7 x 7 x 7 = _____
8. 8 x 8 x 8 = _____
9. 9 x 9 x 9 = _____
10. 10 x 10 x 10 = _____

## Key

| | | | | | |
|---|---|---|---|---|---|
| 216 | B | 3 | T | 125 | E |
| 1 | R | 512 | M | 12 | A |
| 100 | V | 8 | P | 343 | U |
| 729 | O | 218 | F | 27 | U |
| 64 | U | 1,000 | N | 152 | K |

### Riddle Answer:

"Y ___ ___  ___ ___ ___ ___  ___ ___  ___ ___."
9   4    6  7  1  10   8  5    3  2

**NAME** _____

## Riddle 22

# How did the detective find the missing barber?

## What To Do

To find the answer to the riddle, solve the multiplication problems. Then, match each product with a letter in the Key below. Write the correct letters on the blanks below.

**1** 1 x 2 x 3 = _____

**2** 2 x 4 x 1 = _____

**3** 5 x 3 x 4 = _____

**4** 3 x 7 x 3 = _____

**5** 8 x 4 x 5 = _____

**6** 6 x 6 x 7 = _____

**7** 9 x 2 x 5 = _____

**8** 1 x 8 x 7 = _____

**9** 7 x 9 x 5 = _____

**10** 4 x 6 x 4 = _____

## Key

| | | | | | |
|---|---|---|---|---|---|
| 150 . . . . . . . . . V | | 315 . . . . . . . . . N | | 225 . . . . . . . . . A | |
| 8 . . . . . . . . . E | | 252 . . . . . . . . . O | | 63 . . . . . . . . . E | |
| 84 . . . . . . . . . K | | 6 . . . . . . . . . B | | 90 . . . . . . . . . D | |
| 56 . . . . . . . . . W | | 351 . . . . . . . . . Z | | 60 . . . . . . . . . T | |
| 160 . . . . . . . . . H | | 96 . . . . . . . . . T | | 57 . . . . . . . . . X | |

Riddle Answer:  **HE  "COM** ___ ___ ___ **"**  ___ ___ ___ ___  ___ ___ ___ ___ **.**

**1** **4** **7**  **10** **5** **2**  **3** **6** **8** **9**

NAME _____

Riddle 23

# Why did the artist need math?

## What To Do

To find the answer to the riddle, solve the multiplication problems. Then, match each product with a letter in the Key below. Write the correct letters on the blanks below.

**1** $3 \times \frac{1}{2}$ = _____

**2** $5 \times \frac{1}{3}$ = _____

**3** $2 \times \frac{1}{6}$ = _____

**4** $4 \times \frac{2}{5}$ = _____

**5** $3 \times \frac{3}{4}$ = _____

**6** $2 \times \frac{7}{8}$ = _____

**7** $6 \times \frac{6}{9}$ = _____

**8** $5 \times \frac{2}{3}$ = _____

**9** $4 \times \frac{4}{7}$ = _____

**10** $6 \times \frac{9}{11}$ = _____

## Key

| | | | | | |
|---|---|---|---|---|---|
| 3/2 . . . . . . . . . M | | 45/11 . . . . . . . . F | | 10/3 . . . . . . . . . E | |
| 16/7 . . . . . . . . Y | | 9/4 . . . . . . . . . D | | 8/7 . . . . . . . . . G | |
| 6/3 . . . . . . . . . W | | 2/3 . . . . . . . . . Z | | 36/9 . . . . . . . . R | |
| 2/6 . . . . . . . . . N | | 54/11 . . . . . . . U | | 8/5 . . . . . . . . . S | |
| 14/8 . . . . . . . . B | | 3/6 . . . . . . . . . T | | 5/3 . . . . . . . . . B | |

Riddle
Answer: **HE   PAINTE** __  __ __  __ __ __ __ __ __ .
       **5**  **2 9**  **3 10 1 6 8 7 4**

NAME _____

## Riddle 24

# How do birds spread word about their businesses?

## What To Do

To find the answer to the riddle, solve the multiplication problems. Then, match each product with a letter in the Key below. Write the correct letters on the blanks below.

**1** $6 \times \dfrac{5}{6}$ = _____

**2** $8 \times \dfrac{7}{9}$ = _____

**3** $5 \times \dfrac{8}{10}$ = _____

**4** $4 \times \dfrac{11}{12}$ = _____

**5** $7 \times \dfrac{9}{13}$ = _____

**6** $2 \times \dfrac{13}{17}$ = _____

**7** $3 \times \dfrac{12}{15}$ = _____

**8** $9 \times \dfrac{6}{7}$ = _____

**9** $6 \times \dfrac{12}{14}$ = _____

**10** $8 \times \dfrac{14}{19}$ = _____

## Key

| | | | | | |
|---|---|---|---|---|---|
| 30/6 | E | 40/10 | L | 56/9 | S |
| 112/19 | S | 22/19 | G | 62/14 | Z |
| 16/13 | X | 72/14 | F | 24/15 | A |
| 32/15 | B | 54/7 | Y | 63/13 | P |
| 26/17 | T | 36/15 | O | 44/12 | R |

Riddle Answer: **THEY** __ __ __ __  __ __ __ __ __ __ .

**5** **7** **2** **6**  **9** **3** **8** **1** **4** **10**

NAME _____

## Riddle 25

# What did the foot say to the sock?

## What To Do

To find the answer to the riddle, solve the multiplication problems. Simplify your answers.
Then, match each product with a letter in the Key below.
Write the correct letters on the blanks below.

**1** $10 \times \frac{2}{5}$ = _____

**2** $12 \times \frac{1}{2}$ = _____

**3** $15 \times \frac{1}{3}$ = _____

**4** $16 \times \frac{3}{4}$ = _____

**5** $20 \times \frac{4}{5}$ = _____

**6** $18 \times \frac{1}{6}$ = _____

**7** $22 \times \frac{5}{10}$ = _____

**8** $25 \times \frac{3}{5}$ = _____

**9** $30 \times \frac{4}{6}$ = _____

**10** $35 \times \frac{2}{7}$ = _____

## Key

| | | |
|---|---|---|
| 4 .......... C | 70 .......... U | 10 .......... E |
| 3 .......... S | 11 .......... M | 60 .......... I |
| 6 .......... E | 75 .......... W | 16 .......... O |
| 18 .......... N | 20 .......... R | 24 .......... P |
| 5 .......... E | 12 .......... A | 15 .......... V |

Riddle
Answer:    "PLE ___ ___ ___ ___ ___ ___ ___ ___ ___ ___ ___."
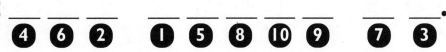
            **4** **6** **2**   **1** **5** **8** **10** **9**   **7** **3**

NAME _____

Riddle 26

# What kind of food always rests?

## What To Do

To find the answer to the riddle, solve the multiplication problems. Then, match each product with a letter in the Key below. Write the correct letters on the blanks below.

**1** $\frac{1}{2} \times \frac{1}{2} =$ _____

**2** $\frac{2}{3} \times \frac{6}{7} =$ _____

**3** $\frac{1}{2} \times \frac{1}{5} =$ _____

**4** $\frac{5}{6} \times \frac{1}{2} =$ _____

**5** $\frac{1}{5} \times \frac{3}{4} =$ _____

**6** $\frac{7}{10} \times \frac{1}{8} =$ _____

**7** $\frac{1}{3} \times \frac{10}{11} =$ _____

**8** $\frac{5}{2} \times \frac{6}{7} =$ _____

**9** $\frac{6}{4} \times \frac{9}{8} =$ _____

**10** $\frac{11}{12} \times \frac{1}{6} =$ _____

## Key

| | | |
|---|---|---|
| 12/6 . . . . . . . . B | 1/10 . . . . . . . . O | 10/33 . . . . . . . . U |
| 54/32 . . . . . . . . T | 12/21 . . . . . . . . T | 3/20 . . . . . . . . A |
| 7/8 . . . . . . . . K | 7/80 . . . . . . . . C | 5/12 . . . . . . . . O |
| 11/72 . . . . . . . . P | 1/5 . . . . . . . . M | 1/4 . . . . . . . . H |
| 18/15 . . . . . . . . L | 30/14 . . . . . . . . O | 1/2 . . . . . . . . E |

Riddle
Answer:    **A  C** ___ ___ ___ ___   ___ ___ ___ ___ ___ ___

NAME _____

## Riddle 27

# What part of Thanksgiving dinner never misses a beat?

## What To Do

To find the answer to the riddle, solve the multiplication problems. Then, match each product with a letter in the Key below. Write the correct letters on the blanks below.

**1**  4 x 0.2 = _____

**2**  7 x 0.3 = _____

**3**  5 x 0.5 = _____

**4**  1 x 0.9 = _____

**5**  6 x 0.4 = _____

**6**  8 x 0.5 = _____

**7**  9 x 0.3 = _____

**8**  5 x 0.2 = _____

**9**  7 x 0.6 = _____

**10**  8 x 0.8 = _____

### Key

| | | |
|---|---|---|
| 2.5 . . . . . . . . . C | 2.1 . . . . . . . . . D | 0.9 . . . . . . . . . R |
| 2.4 . . . . . . . . . E | 1.6 . . . . . . . . . W | 4.2 . . . . . . . . . S |
| 0.25 . . . . . . . . . H | 4.0 . . . . . . . . . M | 6.4 . . . . . . . . . U |
| 0.8 . . . . . . . . . T | 8.0 . . . . . . . . . Q | 1.0 . . . . . . . . . I |
| 24.0 . . . . . . . . . A | 2.7 . . . . . . . . . K | 0.1 . . . . . . . . . G |

Riddle Answer:  **TH** __ "__ __ __ __" __ __ __ __ __

**5**  **2**  **4**  **10**  **6**  **9**  **1**  **8**  **3**  **7**

NAME _____

Riddle 28

# Why did the man step hard on the envelope?

## What To Do

To find the answer to the riddle, solve the multiplication problems. Then, match each product with a letter in the Key below. Write the correct letters on the blanks below.

**1** 10 x 0.4 = _____

**2** 15 x 0.2 = _____

**3** 11 x 0.1 = _____

**4** 12 x 0.5 = _____

**5** 14 x 0.8 = _____

**6** 20 x 0.6 = _____

**7** 19 x 0.4 = _____

**8** 12 x 0.9 = _____

**9** 13 x 0.3 = _____

**10** 17 x 0.8 = _____

## Key

| | | |
|---|---|---|
| 4.0 . . . . . . . . . D | 3.0 . . . . . . . . . A | 1.0 . . . . . . . . F |
| 12.0 . . . . . . . . E | 13.6 . . . . . . . . E | 0.6 . . . . . . . . Z |
| 6.0 . . . . . . . . . P | 1.12 . . . . . . . K | 1.1 . . . . . . . . A |
| 7.6 . . . . . . . . T | 3.9 . . . . . . . . D | 11.2 . . . . . . . . S |
| 0.4 . . . . . . . . N | 10.8 . . . . . . . M | 0.11 . . . . . . . C |

Riddle
Answer:   IT  NE __ __ __ __   __   " __ __ __ __ __ ."

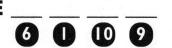

NAME _____

## Riddle 29

# Why did the soccer player hit the ball?

## What To Do

To find the answer to the riddle, solve the multiplication problems. Then, match each product with a letter in the Key below. Write the correct letters on the blanks below.

**1** 0.3 x 0.1 = _____

**2** 0.5 x 0.4 = _____

**3** 0.2 x 0.9 = _____

**4** 0.6 x 0.6 = _____

**5** 0.7 x 0.4 = _____

**6** 0.8 x 0.5 = _____

**7** 0.11 x 0.3 = _____

**8** 0.12 x 0.4 = _____

**9** 0.9 x 0.8 = _____

**10** 0.7 x 0.10 = _____

## Key

| | | | | | |
|---|---|---|---|---|---|
| 0.2 | I | 0.18 | K | 0.048 | K |
| 2.8 | A | 0.28 | S | 0.33 | Z |
| 0.36 | S | 0.03 | T | 0.7 | M |
| 0.4 | R | 4.0 | B | 0.72 | C |
| 0.3 | W | 0.033 | F | 0.07 | O |

Riddle Answer: **JU** __ __ __ __ __ __ __ __ __ __ __
**4** **1**  **7** **10** **6**  **3** **2** **9** **8** **5**

NAME _____

Riddle 30

# How did the chicken leave the farm?

## What To Do

To find the answer to the riddle, solve the multiplication problems. Then, match each product with a letter in the Key below. Write the correct letters on the blanks below.

**1** 0.22 x 0.2 = _____     **6** 0.6 x 0.36 = _____

**2** 0.25 x 0.4 = _____     **7** 0.48 x 0.7 = _____

**3** 0.30 x 0.8 = _____     **8** 0.52 x 0.4 = _____

**4** 0.35 x 0.5 = _____     **9** 0.57 x 0.6 = _____

**5** 0.3 x 0.45 = _____     **10** 0.65 x 0.9 = _____

## Key

| | | |
|---|---|---|
| 0.135 . . . . . . . T | 0.216 . . . . . . . E | 0.1 . . . . . . . . . O |
| 0.112 . . . . . . . X | 0.044 . . . . . . . W | 1.75 . . . . . . . . G |
| 0.175 . . . . . . . C | 0.24 . . . . . . . E | 0.585 . . . . . . . L |
| 0.342 . . . . . . . P | 0.208 . . . . . . . H | 0.44 . . . . . . . . Z |
| 0.363 . . . . . . . A | 0.129 . . . . . . . K | 0.336 . . . . . . . O |

Riddle
Answer:    IT  F __ __ __   __ __ __   __ __ __ __.
              **10** **3** **1**   **5** **8** **6**   **4** **7** **2** **9**

NAME _____

## Riddle 31

# Why did the sick book visit the library?

## What To Do

To find the answer to the riddle, solve the multiplication problems. Then, match each product with a letter in the Key below. Write the correct letters on the blanks below.

**1** How many inches are there in 1 foot? _____

**2** How many inches are there in 2 feet? _____

**3** How many inches are there in 4 feet? _____

**4** How many inches are there in 5 feet? _____

**5** How many inches are there in 7 feet? _____

**6** How many inches are there in 9 feet? _____

**7** How many inches are there in 10 feet? _____

**8** How many inches are there in 6 feet? _____

**9** How many inches are there in 12 feet? _____

**10** How many inches are there in 15 feet? _____

## Key

| | | |
|---|---|---|
| 60 . . . . . . . . . E | 72 . . . . . . . . . D | 88 . . . . . . . . . M |
| 84 . . . . . . . . . C | 140 . . . . . . . . . I | 64 . . . . . . . . . P |
| 180 . . . . . . . . . O | 120 . . . . . . . . . H | 12 . . . . . . . . . U |
| 100 . . . . . . . . . G | 110 . . . . . . . . . L | 24 . . . . . . . . . K |
| 108 . . . . . . . . . T | 144 . . . . . . . . . E | 48 . . . . . . . . . C |

**Riddle Answer:** TO GET " ___ ___ ___ ___ ___ ___ ___  ___ ___ ___ "
                        **3**  **7**  **4**  **5**  **2**  **9**  **8**   **10**  **1**  **6**

NAME _____

Riddle 32

# What do you call a fish standing next to its bowl?

## What To Do

To find the answer to the riddle, solve the multiplication problems. Then, match each product with a letter in the Key below. Write the correct letters on the blanks below.

**1** How many feet are there in 1 yard? _____

**2** How many feet are there in 3 yards? _____

**3** How many feet are there in 6 yards? _____

**4** How many feet are there in 9 yards? _____

**5** How many feet are there in 5 yards? _____

**6** How many feet are there in 10 yards? _____

**7** How many feet are there in 12 yards? _____

**8** How many feet are there in 15 yards? _____

**9** How many feet are there in 20 yards? _____

**10** How many feet are there in 19 yards? _____

## Key

| | | | | | |
|---|---|---|---|---|---|
| 3 | O | 27 | W | 6 | P |
| 9 | A | 45 | F | 30 | O |
| 36 | R | 15 | U | 32 | M |
| 54 | C | 48 | X | 57 | T |
| 60 | E | 18 | T | 35 | G |

Riddle
Answer: **A FISH** __ __ __   __ __   __ __ __ __ __

NAME _____

## Riddle 33

# Where does a king stay when he goes to the beach?

## What To Do

To find the answer to the riddle, solve the multiplication problems. Then, match each product with a letter in the Key below. Write the correct letters on the blanks below.

**1** How many minutes are there in 1 hour? _____

**2** How many minutes are there in 2 hours? _____

**3** How many minutes are there in 4 hours? _____

**4** How many minutes are there in 5 hours? _____

**5** How many minutes are there in 7 hours? _____

**6** How many minutes are there in 10 hours? _____

**7** How many minutes are there in 11 hours? _____

**8** How many minutes are there in 15 hours? _____

**9** How many minutes are there in 18 hours? _____

**10** How many minutes are there in 20 hours? _____

## Key

| | | |
|---|---|---|
| 600 . . . . . . . . S | 1,240 . . . . . . . . M | 900 . . . . . . . . E |
| 420 . . . . . . . . C | 120 . . . . . . . . D | 450 . . . . . . . . B |
| 1,200 . . . . . . . . N | 180 . . . . . . . . X | 1,100 . . . . . . . . I |
| 660 . . . . . . . . S | 300 . . . . . . . . A | 240 . . . . . . . . A |
| 1,080 . . . . . . . . T | 60 . . . . . . . . L | 360 . . . . . . . . O |

Riddle Answer: **A** __ __ __ __ __ __ __ __ __ __

**6** **3** **10** **2**   **5** **4** **7** **9** **1** **8**

NAME _____

Riddle 34

# Why did the shoe go to the doctor?

## What To Do

To find the answer to the riddle, solve the multiplication problems. Then, match each product with a letter in the Key below. Write the correct letters on the blanks below.

**1** How many hours are there in 1 day? _____     **6** How many hours are there in 15 days? _____

**2** How many hours are there in 3 days? _____     **7** How many hours are there in 20 days? _____

**3** How many hours are there in 6 days? _____     **8** How many hours are there in 25 days? _____

**4** How many hours are there in 9 days? _____     **9** How many hours are there in 30 days? _____

**5** How many hours are there in 11 days? _____     **10** How many hours are there in 50 days? _____

## Key

| | | |
|---|---|---|
| 450 . . . . . . . . P | 600 . . . . . . . . G | 144 . . . . . . . . E |
| 264 . . . . . . . . E | 12 . . . . . . . . J | 500 . . . . . . . . M |
| 246 . . . . . . . . N | 24 . . . . . . . . E | 72 . . . . . . . . L |
| 1,200 . . . . . . . . H | 216 . . . . . . . . O | 360 . . . . . . . . T |
| 60 . . . . . . . . K | 720 . . . . . . . . E | 480 . . . . . . . . D |

Riddle
Answer:   T __ __ __ __   " __ __ __ __ __ "  __ __
          **4**  **8** **1** **6**    **10** **5** **9** **2**  **3** **7**

NAME _____

## Riddle 35

# What did the barbell say to the car?

## What To Do

To find the answer to the riddle, solve the multiplication problems. Then, match each product with a letter in the Key below. Write the correct letters on the blanks below.

**1** How many days are there in 1 week? _____

**2** How many days are there in 2 weeks? _____

**3** How many days are there in 3 weeks? _____

**4** How many days are there in 5 weeks? _____

**5** How many days are there in 8 weeks? _____

**6** How many days are there in 10 weeks? _____

**7** How many days are there in 14 weeks? _____

**8** How many days are there in 20 weeks? _____

**9** How many days are there in 25 weeks? _____

**10** How many days are there in 32 weeks? _____

## Key

| | | |
|---|---|---|
| 140 . . . . . . . . . E | 105 . . . . . . . . . G | 65 . . . . . . . . . N |
| 56 . . . . . . . . . P | 21 . . . . . . . . . M | 35 . . . . . . . . . U |
| 14 . . . . . . . . . I | 175 . . . . . . . . . K | 20 . . . . . . . . . A |
| 76 . . . . . . . . . O | 84 . . . . . . . . . J | 70 . . . . . . . . . C |
| 224 . . . . . . . . . P | 7 . . . . . . . . . S | 98 . . . . . . . . . E |

Riddle Answer: "PLEA ___ ___  ___ ___ ___ ___  ___ ___  ___ ___."

NAME _____

## Riddle 36

# What did the sneaker say to the jogger?

## What To Do

To find the answer to the riddle, solve the multiplication problems. Then, match each product with a letter in the Key below. Write the correct letters on the blanks below.

**1** A piece of gum costs 25 cents. How much do 2 pieces of gum cost? _____

**2** A piece of gum costs 25 cents. How much do 4 pieces of gum cost? _____

**3** A bag of pretzels costs $1.00. How much do 3 bags of pretzels cost? _____

**4** A can of soda costs 80 cents. How much do 2 cans of soda cost? _____

**5** A magazine costs $2.50. How much do 3 magazines cost? _____

**6** A box of cookies costs $3.10. How much do 7 boxes of cookies cost? _____

**7** A movie ticket costs $7.50. How much do 5 movie tickets cost? _____

**8** A T-shirt costs $15.00. How much do 6 T-shirts cost? _____

**9** A pair of pants costs $20.00. How much do 8 pairs of pants cost? _____

**10** A pair of shoes costs $30.00. How much do 10 pairs of shoes cost? _____

### Key

| | |
|---|---|
| $300.00 | A |
| $160.00 | T |
| $5.00 | B |
| $1.00 | R |
| $35.70 | S |
| $7.50 | O |
| 25 cents | L |
| $21.70 | U |
| $90.00 | M |
| 75 cents | F |
| $3.00 | E |
| $37.50 | W |
| 50 cents | U |
| $27.10 | P |
| $1.60 | E |

## Riddle Answer:

"YO __ __ __ __ __ __ __ __ __."

6   7   4   10   2   8   3   5   1   9

NAME _____

## Riddle 37

# Where do musicians write music?

## What To Do

To find the answer to the riddle, solve the multiplication problems here. Then, match each product with a letter in the Key below. Write the correct letters on the blanks below.

**1** Joe has 4 one-dollar bills. How much money does he have? _____

**2** Jenna has 3 five-dollar bills. How much money does she have? _____

**3** Henry has 6 ten-dollar bills. How much money does he have? _____

**4** Lisa has 5 twenty-dollar bills. How much money does she have? _____

**5** Jose has 7 one hundred-dollar bills. How much money does he have? _____

**6** Brenda has 1 fifty-dollar bill and 3 one-dollar bills. How much money does she have? _____

**7** John has 4 twenty-dollar bills and 2 five-dollar bills. How much money does he have? _____

**8** Amanda has 8 ten-dollar bills and 2 fifty-dollar bills. How much money does she have? _____

**9** Kevin has 8 five-dollar bills, 1 twenty-dollar bill, and 6 one-dollar bills. How much money does he have? _____

**10** Luisa has 5 five-dollar bills, 2 one hundred-dollar bills, and 4 ten-dollar bills. How much money does she have? _____

### Key

| | | |
|---|---|---|
| $700 | . . . . . . | N |
| $250 | . . . . . . | L |
| $35 | . . . . . . | G |
| $180 | . . . . . . | E |
| $5 | . . . . . | R |
| $66 | . . . . . . | T |
| $170 | . . . . . . | W |
| $90 | . . . . . . | K |
| $265 | . . . . . . | O |
| $15 | . . . . . | B |
| $60 | . . . . . . | N |
| $4 | . . . . . . | O |
| $53 | . . . . . . | O |
| $100 | . . . . . . | S |
| $75 | . . . . . . | M |

## Riddle Answer:

I __ " __ __ __ __ " __ __ __ __

**5**    **3** **1** **9** **8**   **2** **6** **10** **7**   **4**

NAME _____

## Riddle 38

# Why are basketball players messy eaters?

## What To Do

To find the answer to the riddle, solve the multiplication problems. Then, match each product with a letter in the Key below. Write the correct letters on the blanks below.

**1** Alex played in 4 basketball games. He scored 10 points in each game. How many points did Alex score in all? _____

**2** Sheila played in 6 basketball games. She scored 13 points in each game. How many points did Sheila score in all? _____

**3** Jason scored 5 points in a basketball game. Charlie scored 7 times as many points as Jason did. How many points did Charlie score? _____

**4** Selena scored 17 points in a basketball game. Donna scored twice as many points as Selena did. How many points did Donna score? _____

**5** Keith played in 11 basketball games. He scored 9 points in each game. How many points did Keith score in all? _____

**6** Charlene played in 24 basketball games. She scored 12 points in each game. How many points did Charlene score in all? _____

**7** Jodi's basketball team played 10 games. The team scored 50 points in each game. How many points did the team score in all? _____

**8** Larry's basketball team scored 65 points in each game it played. The team played 7 games. How many points did the team score in all? _____

**9** Mark and Kevin played in a basketball game. Mark scored 9 points. Kevin scored 4 times as many points as Mark did. How many points did Kevin score? _____

**10** Keisha played in 4 basketball games. She scored 7 points in the first three games. She scored 10 points in the last game. How many points did Keisha score in all? _____

### Key

| | |
|---|---|
| 500 | L |
| 31 | E |
| 99 | O |
| 40 | L |
| 30 | W |
| 76 | U |
| 36 | B |
| 455 | A |
| 25 | M |
| 35 | T |
| 288 | R |
| 50 | H |
| 78 | B |
| 42 | F |
| 34 | I |

Riddle
Answer:   **THEY  "D** __ __ __ __ __ __ __" __ __ __ __ .
6 4 9 2 1 10   8   7 5 3

NAME _____

## Riddle 39

# How did the square become a triangle?

## What To Do

To find the answer to the riddle, solve the multiplication problems here.
(Don't forget units.)  Then, match each product with a letter in the Key below.
Write the correct letters on the blanks below.

**1** Joe has 2 apples. Tim has 2 times as many apples as Joe has.
How many apples does Tim have? _____

**2** Kendra has 3 books. Paula has 3 times as many books as Kendra has.
How many books does Paula have? _____

**3** Cliff has 5 times as many baseball caps as Wayne has. Wayne has
5 baseball caps. How many baseball caps does Cliff have? _____

**4** Jorge has 10 oranges. Wendy has 2 times as many oranges as
Jorge has. How many oranges does Wendy have? _____

**5** Martha has 6 times as many coats as Russell has. Russell has
5 coats. How many coats does Martha have? _____

**6** Debbie has 9 pairs of shoes. How many shoes does she
have in all? _____

**7** Michael has 8 bunches of bananas. Each bunch has 7 bananas.
How many bananas does he have in all? _____

**8** Leroy has 11 times as many pencils as Renee has. Renee has
11 pencils. How many pencils does Leroy have? _____

**9** Steve has 6 video games. Jack has 8 times as many video
games as Steve has. How many video games do Steve and
Jack have in all? _____

**10** Carla has 7 chairs. Kim has 7 times as many chairs as Carla has.
How many more chairs does Kim have than Carla? _____

### Key

4 apples ...... T
20 oranges .... C
18 shoes ...... N
56 bananas .... C
111 pencils .... I
54 video games  E
48 video games  F
30 coats ...... U
2 apples ...... S
42 chairs ...... A
15 bananas .... K
9 books ...... R
25 caps ...... R
121 pencils .... O
40 coats ...... B

## Riddle Answer:

IT __ __ __  __  __ __ __ __ __ __.

**7** **5** **1**   **10**   **4** **8** **3** **6** **9** **2**

NAME _____

## Riddle 40

# What kind of dessert can you eat for breakfast?

## What To Do

To find the answer to the riddle, solve the multiplication problems. (Don't forget units.)
Then, match each product with a letter in the Key below.
Write the correct letters on the blanks below.

**1** Alice has 10 hats. Juanita has 10 times as many hats as Alice has. How many hats does Juanita have? _____

**2** Gary has 5 pencils. Jose has 30 times as many pencils as Gary has. How many pencils does Jose have? _____

**3** Paul has 15 cookies. Carrie has 20 times as many cookies as Paul has. How many cookies does Carrie have? _____

**4** Dominic has 8 erasers. Peter has 27 times as many erasers as Dominic has. How many erasers does Peter have? _____

**5** Terry has 17 times as many pens as Tam has. Tam has 21 pens. How many pens does Terry have? _____

**6** The library has 50 times as many books as Jackie has. Jackie has 13 books. How many books does the library have? _____

**7** Yuki has 4 cartons of milk in her refrigerator. The supermarket has 75 times as many cartons of milk as Yuki has. How many cartons of milk does the supermarket have? _____

**8** The elephant ate 100 times as many peanuts as Patty ate. Patty ate 23 peanuts. How many peanuts did the elephant eat? _____

### Key

| | |
|---|---|
| 500 cookies | U |
| 100 hats | S |
| 3,200 peanuts | M |
| 200 cartons | I |
| 357 pens | N |
| 140 pencils | W |
| 300 cookies | K |
| 150 pencils | A |
| 224 erasers | G |
| 650 books | P |
| 216 erasers | C |
| 120 hats | F |
| 2,300 peanuts | A |
| 560 books | D |
| 300 cartons | E |

Riddle
Answer:

___ ___ ___ " ___ ___ ___ ___ ___ "
**6** **2** **5** **4** **8** **3** **7** **1**

# Answers

**Page 5: Multiplying by 1's and 2's**
1. 5
2. 8
3. 11
4. 26
5. 6
6. 10
7. 12
8. 16
9. 18
10. 24

*What did the rocket say when it left the party?*
**"Time to take off."**

**Page 6: Multiplying by 3's**
1. 15
2. 6
3. 24
4. 12
5. 27
6. 18
7. 30
8. 36
9. 33
10. 0

*What did the owl say when someone knocked on its door?*
**"Whoooo is it?"**

**Page 7: Multiplying by 4's**
1. 12
2. 24
3. 8
4. 36
5. 28
6. 40
7. 32
8. 52
9. 4
10. 48

*What does a basketball player never have to pay for?*
**A "free" throw**

**Page 8: Multiplying by 5's**
1. 20
2. 30
3. 50
4. 40
5. 60
6. 75
7. 100
8. 125
9. 150
10. 25

*What always has an eye out for entertainment?*
**Tele"vision"**

**Page 9: Multiplying by 6's**
1. 12
2. 48
3. 24
4. 60
5. 90
6. 18
7. 54
8. 72
9. 42
10. 120

*Why did the car make so much noise?*
**It had a motor mouth.**

**Page 10: Multiplying by 7's**
1. 42
2. 70
3. 49
4. 84
5. 56
6. 35
7. 14
8. 77
9. 21
10. 63

*Why did the puppy fall asleep?*
**It was dog tired.**

**Page 11: Multiplying by 8's**
1. 16
2. 48
3. 24
4. 64
5. 32
6. 80
7. 72
8. 40
9. 112
10. 88

*What kind of pie do ghosts like best?*
**"Boo"berry pie**

**Page 12: Multiplying by 9's**
1. 90
2. 9
3. 36
4. 117
5. 72
6. 81
7. 54
8. 45
9. 63
10. 180

*Why did the dog chew up the wooden table leg?*
**It wanted some "bark."**

**Page 13: Multiplying by 10's and 100's**
1. 40
2. 70
3. 100
4. 120
5. 360
6. 1,400
7. 600
8. 3,000
9. 5,000
10. 7,500

*What should you take on a trip to the desert?*
**A "thirst"-aid kit**

# Answers

**Page 14: Multiplying a Number by Itself**
1. 1
2. 4
3. 9
4. 16
5. 25
6. 36
7. 49
8. 64
9. 81

*What are a bandit's favorite fruits?*
**Bad apples**

**Page 15: Multiplying a Number by Itself**
1. 100
2. 121
3. 144
4. 169
5. 196
6. 225
7. 256
8. 289
9. 324
10. 361

*What kinds of food are popular at the beach?*
**"Sand"wiches**

**Page 16: 2-Digit Numbers x 1-Digit Numbers**
1. 180
2. 300
3. 400
4. 160
5. 210
6. 560
7. 810
8. 90
9. 175

*Where did the turkey, ham, and roast beef go to party?*
**A "meat"ball**

**Page 17: 2-Digit Numbers x 1-Digit Numbers**
1. 30
2. 42
3. 65
4. 77
5. 72
6. 48
7. 80
8. 38
9. 119
10. 120

*What did the doctor say to the patient who swallowed a roll of film?*
**"Hope nothing develops."**

**Page 18: 3-Digit Numbers x 1-Digit Numbers**
1. 1,600
2. 2,400
3. 1,500
4. 900
5. 4,800
6. 1,800
7. 2,800
8. 4,000
9. 3,500
10. 2,700

*Why do spiders use computers?*
**To visit "web" sites**

**Page 19: 3-Digit Numbers x 1-Digit Numbers**
1. 330
2. 640
3. 1,320
4. 500
5. 2,310
6. 2,720
7. 3,780
8. 2,250

*What kind of cat is the life of the party?*
**A "wild"cat**

**Page 20: 3-Digit Numbers x 1-Digit Numbers**
1. 111
2. 1,080
3. 1,484
4. 1,134
5. 1,530
6. 2,856
7. 4,176
8. 1,528
9. 1,538
10. 1,941

*Why did the bowling pins lie down?*
**They went on "strike."**

**Page 21: 3-Digit Numbers x 2-Digit Numbers**
1. 2,300
2. 3,400
3. 9,300
4. 17,600
5. 9,500
6. 16,200
7. 24,500
8. 14,400
9. 45,000

*What are the cheapest ships to buy?*
**"Sale"boats**

**Page 22: 4-Digit Numbers x 1-Digit Numbers**
1. 8,000
2. 4,500
3. 7,200
4. 10,400
5. 28,500
6. 2,250
7. 46,200
8. 13,020
9. 10,620
10. 43,100

*What do pigs want for dessert?*
**Lots of mud pies**

# Answers

**Page 23: 4-Digit Numbers x 1-Digit Numbers**
1. 6,690
2. 18,584
3. 7,156
4. 27,189
5. 22,380
6. 39,284
7. 48,528
8. 24,378
9. 22,356
10. 44,346

*What kind of dog loves to take baths?*
**A "shampoo"dle**

**Page 24: 4-Digit Numbers x 2-Digit Numbers**
1. 11,000
2. 24,000
3. 30,000
4. 56,000
5. 100,000
6. 144,000
7. 210,000
8. 256,000
9. 360,000
10. 375,000

*Why did the spider join the baseball team?*
**To catch "flies"**

**Page 25: Multiplying Three Numbers**
1. 1
2. 8
3. 27
4. 64
5. 125
6. 216
7. 343
8. 512
9. 729
10. 1,000

*What did the candle say to the match?*
**"You burn me up."**

**Page 26: Multiplying Three Numbers**
1. 6
2. 8
3. 60
4. 63
5. 160
6. 252
7. 90
8. 56
9. 315
10. 96

*How did the detective find the missing barber?*
**He "combed" the town.**

**Page 27: Fractions**
1. $\frac{3}{2}$
2. $\frac{5}{3}$
3. $\frac{2}{6}$
4. $\frac{8}{5}$
5. $\frac{9}{4}$
6. $\frac{14}{8}$
7. $\frac{36}{9}$
8. $\frac{10}{3}$
9. $\frac{16}{7}$
10. $\frac{54}{11}$

*Why did the artist need math?*
**He painted by numbers.**

**Page 28: Fractions**
1. $\frac{30}{6}$
2. $\frac{56}{9}$
3. $\frac{40}{10}$
4. $\frac{44}{12}$
5. $\frac{63}{13}$
6. $\frac{26}{17}$
7. $\frac{36}{15}$
8. $\frac{54}{7}$
9. $\frac{72}{14}$
10. $\frac{112}{19}$

*How do birds spread word about their businesses?*
**They post flyers.**

**Page 29: Fractions**
1. 4
2. 6
3. 5
4. 12
5. 16
6. 3
7. 11
8. 15
9. 20
10. 10

*What did the foot say to the sock?*
**"Please cover me."**

**Page 30: Fractions**
1. $\frac{1}{4}$
2. $\frac{12}{21}$
3. $\frac{1}{10}$
4. $\frac{5}{12}$
5. $\frac{3}{20}$
6. $\frac{7}{80}$
7. $\frac{10}{33}$
8. $\frac{30}{14}$
9. $\frac{54}{32}$
10. $\frac{11}{72}$

*What kind of food always rests?*
**A couch potato**

**Page 31: Decimals**
1. 0.8
2. 2.1
3. 2.5
4. 0.9
5. 2.4
6. 4.0
7. 2.7
8. 1.0
9. 4.2
10. 6.4

*What part of Thanksgiving dinner never misses a beat?*
**The "drum"stick**

# Answers

## Page 32: Decimals
| | | | |
|---|---|---|---|
| 1. | 4.0 | 6. | 12.0 |
| 2. | 3.0 | 7. | 7.6 |
| 3. | 1.1 | 8. | 10.8 |
| 4. | 6.0 | 9. | 3.9 |
| 5. | 11.2 | 10. | 13.6 |

*Why did the man step hard on the envelope?*
**It needed a "stamp."**

## Page 33: Decimals
| | | | |
|---|---|---|---|
| 1. | 0.03 | 6. | 0.4 |
| 2. | 0.2 | 7. | 0.033 |
| 3. | 0.18 | 8. | 0.048 |
| 4. | 0.36 | 9. | 0.72 |
| 5. | 0.28 | 10. | 0.07 |

*Why did the soccer player hit the ball?*
**Just for kicks**

## Page 34: Decimals
| | | | |
|---|---|---|---|
| 1. | 0.044 | 6. | 0.216 |
| 2. | 0.1 | 7. | 0.336 |
| 3. | 0.24 | 8. | 0.208 |
| 4. | 0.175 | 9. | 0.342 |
| 5. | 0.135 | 10. | 0.585 |

*How did the chicken leave the farm?*
**It flew the coop.**

## Page 35: Measurement
| | | | |
|---|---|---|---|
| 1. | 12 | 6. | 108 |
| 2. | 24 | 7. | 120 |
| 3. | 48 | 8. | 72 |
| 4. | 60 | 9. | 144 |
| 5. | 84 | 10. | 180 |

*Why did the sick book visit the library?*
**To get "checked out"**

## Page 36: Measurement
| | | | |
|---|---|---|---|
| 1. | 3 | 6. | 30 |
| 2. | 9 | 7. | 36 |
| 3. | 18 | 8. | 45 |
| 4. | 27 | 9. | 60 |
| 5. | 15 | 10. | 57 |

*What do you call a fish standing next to its fishbowl?*
**A fish out of water**

## Page 37: Time
| | | | |
|---|---|---|---|
| 1. | 60 | 6. | 600 |
| 2. | 120 | 7. | 660 |
| 3. | 240 | 8. | 900 |
| 4. | 300 | 9. | 1,080 |
| 5. | 420 | 10. | 1,200 |

*Where does a king stay when he goes to the beach?*
**A sand castle**

## Page 38: Time
| | | | |
|---|---|---|---|
| 1. | 24 | 6. | 360 |
| 2. | 72 | 7. | 480 |
| 3. | 144 | 8. | 600 |
| 4. | 216 | 9. | 720 |
| 5. | 264 | 10. | 1,200 |

*Why did the shoe go to the doctor?*
**To get "heel"ed**

## Page 39: Time
| | | | |
|---|---|---|---|
| 1. | 7 | 6. | 70 |
| 2. | 14 | 7. | 98 |
| 3. | 21 | 8. | 140 |
| 4. | 35 | 9. | 175 |
| 5. | 56 | 10. | 224 |

*What did the barbell say to the car?*
**"Please pick me up."**

## Page 40: Word Problems
| | | | |
|---|---|---|---|
| 1. | 50 cents | 6. | $21.70 |
| 2. | $1.00 | 7. | $37.50 |
| 3. | $3.00 | 8. | $90.00 |
| 4. | $1.60 | 9. | $160.00 |
| 5. | $7.50 | 10. | $300.00 |

*What did the sneaker say to the jogger?*
**"You wear me out."**

## Page 41: Word Problems
| | | | |
|---|---|---|---|
| 1. | $4 | 6. | $53 |
| 2. | $15 | 7. | $90 |
| 3. | $60 | 8. | $180 |
| 4. | $100 | 9. | $66 |
| 5. | $700 | 10. | $265 |

*Where do musicians write music?*
**In "note"books**

## Page 42: Word Problems
| | | | |
|---|---|---|---|
| 1. | 40 | 6. | 288 |
| 2. | 78 | 7. | 500 |
| 3. | 35 | 8. | 455 |
| 4. | 34 | 9. | 36 |
| 5. | 99 | 10. | 31 |

*Why are basketball players messy eaters?*
**They "dribble" a lot.**

## Page 43: Word Problems
1. 4 apples
2. 9 books
3. 25 caps
4. 20 oranges
5. 30 coats
6. 18 shoes
7. 56 bananas
8. 121 pencils
9. 54 video games
10. 42 chairs

*How did the square become a triangle?*
**It cut a corner.**

## Page 44: Word Problems
1. 100 hats
2. 150 pencils
3. 300 cookies
4. 216 erasers
5. 357 pens
6. 650 books
7. 300 cartons
8. 2,300 peanuts

*What kind of dessert can you eat for breakfast?*
**Pan"cakes"**